WallQuilts for All

Transform your walls from barren to beautiful with quilted wall hangings! This generous assortment includes 12 designs that are so diverse, you're sure to want to make them not only for yourself but for family and friends, as well. Accent a craft room with a sewing sampler, or brighten the nursery with a design that's as "cute as a button." A wildlife wall hanging will spruce up a cabin retreat, or hang it in the den for a taste of the Great Outdoors. Our seasonal and holiday themes will keep your walls festively decorated throughout the year. Buttons and other embellishments add dimensional interest to these pretty-as-a-picture wall quilts.

PRINTED WITH SOY INK

Made in U.S.A.

ISBN 1-57486-761-X

WARM HANDS, WARM HEART
Finished Size: 13^1/$_2$" x 15^1/$_2$"

Basic Tools and Supplies (see page 26)

Fabrics
- ^{1}/$_3$ yd tan muslin (31 cm)
- ^{1}/$_8$ yd red and gold print (12 cm)
- ^{1}/$_8$ yd gold solid (12 cm)
- ^{1}/$_4$ yd mitten novelty print (23 cm)
- ^{1}/$_2$ yd backing (46 cm)
- Small pieces of red, blue, green, and gold prints

Other Supplies
- Black embroidery floss
- Batting
- 26" of 2mm black twisted cotton cord
- Black sewing thread
- Small piece ecru plush felt or fur trim
- Permanent fabric adhesive
- Eight miniature spring clothespins
- Two ^{3}/$_4$" dia. plastic rings

Read Basic Instructions, pages 27-29.

Block and Border Preparation
- On tan muslin, draw an 8^1/$_2$" x 10^1/$_2$" rectangle with pencil for center block.
- From red and gold print, cut two 1^1/$_4$" x 8^1/$_2$" strips for short inner borders and two 1^1/$_4$" x 12" strips for long inner borders.
- From gold solid, cut two ^{3}/$_4$" x 10" strips for short center borders and two ^{3}/$_4$" x 12^1/$_2$" strips for long center borders.
- From mitten print, cut two 2^1/$_4$" x 10^1/$_2$" strips for short outer borders and two 2^1/$_4$" x 16" strips for long outer borders.

Embroidery
1. Draw a line with air soluble pen 1^7/$_8$" down from pencil line at top of muslin and 1" up from bottom pencil line. Using pattern on page 30, center and trace words on these lines.
2. Backstitch letters with two strands of floss. Cut out embroidered block on pencil lines.

Borders
When sewing, always match right sides and raw edges and use a ^{1}/$_4$" seam allowance.
1. Sew short inner borders to each side of center block. Sew long inner borders to top and bottom of center block.
2. Repeat with center borders and again with outer borders to complete wall hanging top.

Finishing
1. Cut batting and backing the same size as wall hanging top. Sew wall hanging together.
2. Quilt in the ditch around center block, inner borders, and center borders.
3. Tie a knot at each end of black cord. Tie a bow at each end of cord, 3" from ends. Place each bow about 2^1/$_2$" down from top corners of center block. Middle of cord should curve downward slightly between bows. Adjust bow size if necessary to fit. Tack bow centers in place and couch cord to background with black sewing thread.
4. For each mitten, fuse two 2" x 2^1/$_2$" pieces of fabric, wrong sides together, with a same-size piece of fusible web. Using pattern on page 30, cut one mitten from each print fabric. Trace heart pattern on page 30 and make four heart appliqués of same prints. Fuse hearts to mittens. Cut four ^{5}/$_8$" x 1^1/$_2$" strips from felt or fur, rounding corners. Glue to top front of each mitten.
5. Attach two clothespins to top of each mitten as shown in photo. Apply fabric adhesive to back of each clothespin and position on cord, spacing mittens evenly across cord.
6. Sew one plastic ring to each top corner of wall hanging on back, being careful not to sew all the way through to the front of the wall hanging.

FRIENDSHIP HEARTS

Finished Size: 15" x 15"

Basic Tools and Supplies (see page 26)

Fabrics
- $^1/_4$ yd tan muslin (23 cm)
- Small pieces of eight assorted tan prints
- $^1/_8$ yd small red check (12 cm)
- $^1/_4$ yd large red check (23 cm)
- Small pieces of eight assorted red prints
- $^1/_2$ yd backing (46 cm)

Other Supplies
- Black embroidery floss
- Batting
- Eight assorted $^1/_2$" – $^7/_8$" dia. tan buttons
- Two $^3/_4$" dia. plastic rings

Read Basic Instructions, pages 27-29.

Block and Border Preparation
- On tan muslin, draw a $5^1/_2$" square with pencil for center block.
- From assorted tan prints, cut four 3" squares and four 3" x $5^1/_2$" rectangles for heart blocks.
- From small red check, cut two 1" x $10^1/_2$" strips for short inner borders and two 1" x $11^1/_2$" strips for long inner borders.
- From large red check, cut two $2^1/_2$" x $11^1/_2$" strips for short outer borders and two $2^1/_2$" x $15^1/_2$" strips for long outer borders.

Embroidery and Appliqués
1. Use pattern on page 31 to center and trace words on muslin square.
2. Backstitch letters with two strands of floss; work French knots for dots. Cut out embroidered block on pencil lines.
3. Use patterns on page 31 to make four small hearts, two wide hearts, and two long hearts from eight red prints. Referring to photo, fuse one heart to each tan square and rectangle.
4. Blanket stitch around each heart appliqué with two strands of floss.

Piecing and Borders
When sewing, always match right sides and raw edges and use a $^1/_4$" seam allowance.
1. Arrange appliqué blocks as shown in photo with lettered block in center.
2. Sew blocks together as follows:
   - Sew 1, 2, and 3 together to make top row.
   - Sew 4 to 5, 6 to 7, and 8 to 9.
   - Sew 4-5 to 6-7 to make a square.
   - Sew 8-9 to side of square to make a rectangle.
   - Sew top row (1-2-3) to top of rectangle to complete center block.

3. Sew one short inner border to each side of pieced center block. Sew one long inner border to top and bottom of center block. Repeat with outer borders to complete wall hanging top.

Finishing
1. Cut batting and backing the same size as wall hanging top. Sew wall hanging together.
2. Quilt in the ditch around center block, inner borders, and each pieced block.
3. Sew a button to the center of each heart.
4. Sew one plastic ring to each top corner of wall hanging on back, being careful not to sew all the way through to the front of the wall hanging.

SIMPLE LIFE

Finished Size: 13¹/₂" x 16"

Basic Tools and Supplies (see page 26)

Fabrics
- ¹/₄ yd white weaver's cloth (23 cm)
- Small pieces of light green, blue, yellow, and pink prints
- ¹/₈ yd yellow check (12 cm)
- ¹/₄ yd blue floral print (23 cm)
- Small pieces of assorted fabrics for appliqués, flowers, and leaves
- ¹/₂ yd backing (46 cm)

Other Supplies
- Black and green embroidery floss
- Batting
- ¹/₂" dia. white shank-style button
- Three ⁷/₁₆" dia. white buttons
- Three ⁵/₈" dia. white buttons
- Yellow sewing thread
- 3mm dia. black bead
- 1³/₄" tall wooden split pot
- ⁷/₈" tall wooden wren egg
- 1³/₈" tall wooden bird
- Terra cotta, yellow, black, blue, and gold acrylic paints
- Permanent fabric adhesive
- Two ³/₄" dia. plastic rings

Read Basic Instructions, pages 27-29.

Block and Border Preparation
- On white weaver's cloth, draw a 3¹/₂" x 5" rectangle with pencil for center block.
- From light green and blue prints, cut one 3¹/₂" x 8¹/₂" block each. From yellow and pink prints, cut one 3" x 5" block each.
- From yellow check, cut two 1¹/₄" x 8¹/₂" strips for short inner borders and two 1¹/₄" x 12¹/₂" strips for long inner borders.
- From blue floral print, cut two 2¹/₂" x 10" strips for short outer borders and two 2¹/₂" x 16¹/₂" strips for long outer borders.

Embroidery and Appliqués
1. Use pattern on page 32 to trace words onto center of white block.

2. Backstitch letters with two strands of black floss; work French knots for dots. Cut out embroidered block on pencil lines.
3. Reverse rabbit pattern on page 32. Use birdhouse and bee wing patterns on page 32 and the reversed rabbit pattern to make appliqués. Fuse in place on blocks.
4. Trace flower stems onto flowerpot and birdhouse blocks. Use three strands of green floss to backstitch stems and work lazy daisy stitch leaves on pole.

Piecing and Borders
When sewing, always match right sides and raw edges and use a ¹/₄" seam allowance.
1. Referring to photo, sew bee and rabbit blocks to the top and bottom of the center block to make one vertical row. Sew the flowerpot block to the left and the birdhouse block to the right of the pieced row to complete the center block.
2. Using pattern on page 32, trace the bee antennae and path onto the bee block, extending the line down into the flowerpot block where a flower will be positioned. Use two strands of black floss to backstitch bee's antennae with a French knot at each tip. Use three strands of black floss and a running stitch to embroider the bee path.
3. Sew one short inner border to each side of center block. Sew one long inner border to top and bottom of center block. Repeat with outer borders to complete wall hanging top.

Finishing
1. Cut batting and backing the same size as wall hanging top. Sew wall hanging together.
2. Quilt in the ditch around center block, inner borders, and each pieced block.
3. For rabbit tail, cut a 1" circle from fabric. Sew running stitches around edge. Place shank button on wrong side of circle and pull thread to cover button. Sew to rabbit for tail.
4. To make yo-yo flowers, use pattern on page 33. Cut one circle each from blue, yellow, and pink prints. Fold raw edge of each circle ¹/₈" to wrong side. Using matching thread, sew running stitches around entire circle near folded edge. With right side of fabric facing

out, pull thread to tightly gather fabric; knot thread to secure. Flatten yo-yo so that gathered circle is at the center; sew $5/8$" button over hole with thread to match yo-yo. Sew each button and flower to wall hanging, positioning as shown in photo.

5. For leaves, trace pattern on page 33 onto wrong side of fabric four times. Fold fabric in half, right sides facing, and sew on traced lines. Cut out $1/4$" from seam; clip curves and points. Make a slash **through one layer only** as indicated on pattern; turn right side out and press. Hand gather and fold each leaf set; glue leaf sets to flowers, tucking center under flower. Reserve last set for pot.

6. Using yellow thread, sew small white buttons to vine along birdhouse pole.

7. Sew black bead to rabbit for eye.

8. Paint wooden pieces as follows:
   • split pot — terra cotta
   • bee (wren egg) — yellow with black stripes and a black dot for eye
   • bird — blue with gold beak

Outline bird and dot bird eye with permanent marker.

9. Hand gather, fold, and glue remaining leaf set inside pot so leaves are extending out the top. Glue pot to bottom of flower stem.

10. Glue bird and bee in place.

11. Sew one plastic ring to each top corner of wall hanging on back, being careful not to sew all the way through to the front of the wall hanging.

ONE NATION EVERMORE

Finished Size: 12¹/₂" x 14"

Basic Tools and Supplies (see page 26)

Fabrics
- ¹/₄ yd natural osnaburg (23 cm)
- ¹/₄ yd red print (23 cm)
- ¹/₄ yd blue print (23 cm)
- Small piece gold print
- ¹/₂ yd backing (46 cm)

Other Supplies
- Black embroidery floss
- Batting
- Five ⁵/₈" dia. tan buttons
- Four ⁷/₈" dia. tan buttons
- 1¹/₂" x 14¹/₂" wooden slat
- Wood stain
- Two 3³/₄" tall wooden stars
- Gold acrylic paint
- Tacky craft glue
- Two small sawtooth hangers

Read Basic Instructions, pages 27-29.

Block and Border Preparation
- On natural osnaburg, draw a 7¹/₂" x 9" rectangle with pencil for center block.
- From red print, cut two 1¹/₄" x 7¹/₂" strips for short side borders, two 1¹/₄" x 10¹/₂" strips for long inner borders, and two 6" x 9" rectangles for hanging tabs.
- From blue print, cut two 2¹/₂" x 9" strips for short outer borders and two 2¹/₂" x 14¹/₂" strips for long outer borders.

Embroidery
1. Use pattern on page 33 to trace words onto osnaburg.
2. Backstitch verse with three strands of embroidery floss; work French knot for dot. Backstitch name with one strand; work French knots for dots. Cut out embroidered block on pencil lines.

Borders and Appliqués
When sewing, always match right sides and raw edges and use a ¹/₄" seam allowance.
1. Sew one short inner border to each side of center block. Sew one long inner border to top and bottom of center block. Repeat with outer borders.
2. Reverse patterns on page 34 to make star appliqués. Referring to photo, position star #1 in top right corner and continue clockwise around block with other stars in numerical order. Fuse appliqués in place.

Finishing
1. Cut batting and backing the same size as wall hanging top. Sew wall hanging together.
2. Quilt in the ditch around center block, inner borders, and each star.
3. Sew a small tan button to the center of each star.
4. Make hanging tabs from red print rectangles. Attach to top of wall hanging with large tan buttons.
5. Apply wood stain to wooden slat following manufacturer's instructions. Attach sawtooth hangers to back of slat at each end. Paint stars gold. Draw small "stitches" around the edge of each star with permanent marker. Glue one star to each end of slat. Glue large tan button to center of each star. Slip hanger through tabs.

One flag, one land
One heart, one hand
One nation
    Evermore

O.W. Holmes

Basic Tools and Supplies (see page 26)

Fabrics
- ¹/₃ yd tan osnaburg (31 cm)
- ¹/₄ yd mottled green (23 cm)
- ¹/₄ yd gold plaid homespun (23 cm)
- ¹/₈ yd muted fall-colored fabric (12 cm)
- Small piece each of medium and dark brown prints
- ¹/₂ yd backing (46 cm)

Other Supplies
- Black and brown embroidery floss
- Batting
- Two ³/₄" dia. plastic rings

Read Basic Instructions, pages 27-29.

Block and Border Preparation
- On tan osnaburg, draw an 8¹/₂" x 14¹/₂" rectangle with pencil for center block.
- From mottled green fabric, cut two 1¹/₄" x 10" strips for short inner borders, two 1¹/₄" x 14¹/₂" strips for long inner borders, two 1" x 15" strips for short outer borders, and two 1" x 20" strips for long outer borders.
- From gold plaid homespun, cut two 2¹/₂" x 14" strips for short center borders and two 2¹/₂" x 16" strips for long center borders.

Embroidery and Appliqués
1. Use patterns on pages 36 and 37 to trace words onto top left corner and bottom right corner of osnaburg rectangle. Trace stem down center of block.

2. Using three strands of black floss, backstitch letters. Use four strands of brown floss and a stem stitch to embroider stem.
3. Reverse leaf and acorn patterns on pages 36 and 37 and make leaf and acorn appliqués. Position acorns and top four leaves along stem and fuse in place. Reserve bottom leaf until borders are added.
4. Cut out embroidered block on pencil lines.

Borders
When sewing, always match right sides and raw edges and use a ¹/₄" seam allowance.
1. Sew one short inner border to each side of center block. Sew one long inner border to top and bottom of center block.
2. Repeat with center borders and again with outer borders to complete wall hanging top.

Finishing
1. Fuse last leaf into position, overlapping inner border.
2. Blanket stitch around each leaf and acorn with two strands of brown floss.
3. Cut batting and backing the same size as wall hanging top. Sew wall hanging together.
4. Quilt in the ditch around center block, inner borders, and center borders. Quilt around each leaf with a longer stitch.
5. Sew one plastic ring to each top corner of wall hanging on back, being careful not to sew all the way through to the front of the wall hanging.

BATTY HALLOWEEN

Finished Size: 15" x 16"

Basic Tools and Supplies (see page 26)

Fabrics
- $1/3$ yd tan weaver's cloth (31 cm)
- $1/4$ yd orange print (23 cm)
- $1/4$ yd black Halloween print (23 cm)
- $1/8$ yd yellow print (12 cm)
- Small piece of black solid
- $1/2$ yd backing (46 cm)

Other Supplies
- Black embroidery floss
- Batting
- Two $1/4$" dia. black buttons
- Two $1^1/8$" dia. black buttons
- $1^1/2$" x 18" wooden slat
- Two $2^1/4$"w wooden pumpkins
- Two $1^5/8$"w wooden bats
- Black, orange, green, and white acrylic paints
- Tacky craft glue
- Two small sawtooth hangers

Read Basic Instructions, pages 27-29.

Block and Border Preparation
- On weaver's cloth, draw a $9^1/2$" x $10^1/2$" rectangle with pencil for center block.
- From orange print, cut two 1" x $9^1/2$" strips for short inner borders, two 1" x $11^1/2$" strips for long inner borders, and two $5^1/2$" x 9" rectangles for hanging tabs.
- From black Halloween print, cut two $2^1/2$" x $10^1/2$" strips for short center borders and two $2^1/2$" x $15^1/2$" strips for long center borders.
- From yellow print, cut two 1" x $14^1/2$" strips for short outer borders and two 1" x $16^1/2$" strips for long outer borders.

Embroidery and Appliqués
1. Use patterns on pages 38 and 39 to trace words on weaver's cloth.
2. Backstitch words with two strands of floss; work straight stitches for dot.
3. Use bat body, wing, legs, eyes, and teeth patterns on pages 38 and 39 to make appliqué pieces. Eyes and teeth are cut from a doubled piece of scrap weaver cloth. Fuse appliqués in place.
4. Cut out embroidered block on pencil lines.

Borders
When sewing, always match right sides and raw edges and use a $1/4$" seam allowance.
1. Sew one short inner border to each side of center block. Sew one long inner border to top and bottom of center block.
2. Repeat with center borders and again with outer borders to complete wall hanging top.

Finishing
1. Cut batting and backing the same size as wall hanging top. Sew wall hanging together.
2. Quilt in the ditch around center block, inner borders, and center borders.
3. Sew small black buttons to eyes.
4. Make hanging tabs from orange rectangles. Attach to top of wall hanging with large black buttons.
5. Paint wooden pieces as follows:
   - slat — black
   - pumpkins — orange with green stems
   - bats — black with two white dots for eyes
   Outline pumpkins with permanent marker.
6. Attach sawtooth hangers to back of slat at each end. Glue one pumpkin to each end of slat. Glue a bat to each pumpkin. Slip slat through hanging tabs.

LOVING HOME

Finished Size: 13" x 17"

Basic Tools and Supplies (see page 26)

Fabrics
- ¹/₄ yd white weaver's cloth (23 cm)
- ¹/₄ yd black and white print (23 cm)
- ¹/₈ yd red solid (12 cm)
- ¹/₄ yd black and white checked homespun (23 cm)
- Small pieces of gold and blue solids
- ¹/₂ yd backing (46 cm)

Other Supplies
- Black embroidery floss
- Batting
- Three ¹/₄" dia. black buttons
- Two 1¹/₈" dia. red buttons
- 1¹/₂" x 18" wooden slat
- Two 3³/₈" x 2³/₈" wooden hearts
- White and red acrylic paints
- Tacky craft glue
- Two sawtooth hangers

Read Basic Instructions, pages 27-29.

Block and Border Preparation
- On white weaver's cloth, draw a 7¹/₂" x 11¹/₂" rectangle with pencil for center block.
- From black and white print, cut two 1¹/₄" x 7¹/₂" strips for short inner borders, two 1¹/₄" x 13" strips for long inner borders, and two 6" x 9" rectangles for hanging tabs.
- From red solid, cut two ³/₄" x 9" strips for short center borders and two ³/₄" x 13¹/₂" strips for long center borders.
- From black and white homespun, cut two 2¹/₂" x 9¹/₂" strips for short outer borders and two 2¹/₂" x 17¹/₂" strips for long outer borders.

Embroidery and Appliqués
1. Use patterns on page 35 to center and trace words and houses on white center block.
2. Backstitch letters with two strands of floss; make French knots for dots. Backstitch house outlines with three strands of floss. Sew a running stitch for smoke tendrils with two strands of floss.
3. Use heart, window, and door patterns on page 35 to make appliqués. Fuse appliqués to center house as shown in photo.
4. Backstitch around heart, door, and window appliqués with three strands of floss; make lines through window for panes. Cut out embroidered block on pencil lines.

Borders
When sewing, always match right sides and raw edges and use a ¹/₄" seam allowance.
1. Sew one short inner border to each side of center block. Sew one long inner border to top and bottom of center block.
2. Repeat with center borders and again with outer borders to complete wall hanging top.

Finishing
1. Cut batting and backing the same size as wall hanging top. Sew wall hanging together.
2. Quilt in the ditch around center block, inner borders, and center borders.
3. Sew a black button to each door for doorknob.
4. Make hanging tabs from black and white print rectangles. Attach to top of wall hanging with red buttons.
5. Paint slat white and wooden hearts red. Attach sawtooth hangers to back of slat at each end. Glue one heart to front of slat at each end. Slip hanger through tabs.

WILD ABOUT WILDLIFE

Finished Size: 17" x 17"

Basic Tools and Supplies (see page 26)

Fabric

- Small pieces of natural and tea bag osnaburg
- Small pieces of assorted brown, green, and blue plaid homespun
- ¼ yd dark red (23 cm)
- ¼ yd brown plaid (23 cm)
- ¼ yd black plaid (23 cm)
- Small pieces of assorted fabrics for appliqués
- ⅝ yd backing (58 cm)

Other Supplies

- Black, brown, white, blue, red, green, gold, and ecru embroidery floss
- Ecru cord or pearl cotton
- Batting
- Silver fishing lure with fish shape (about 2¼" long)
- Permanent fabric adhesive
- Silver earring hook
- 3mm dia. black bead
- Twig for tree (about ³/₁₆" diameter, 4" long)
- 2¼" long wooden bear
- 1½" long wooden fish
- 3½" x 1" wooden canoe
- Medium and dark brown, tan, light and medium green, cream, black, and white acrylic paints
- Two 1⅛" dia. tan buttons
- Two small sawtooth hangers
- Branch (about ⅝" diameter, 20" long, fairly straight)

Read Basic Instructions, pages 27-29.

Block and Border Preparation

- On natural osnaburg, draw two 3½" x 6½" rectangles for lettered blocks.
- On tea bag osnaburg, draw a 3½" and a 6½" square for lettered blocks.
- From assorted homespun fabrics, cut five 3½" squares and one 3½" x 6½" rectangle.
- From dark red, cut two 1" x 12½" strips for short inner borders and two 1" x 13½" strips for long inner borders.
- From brown plaid, cut two 2½" x 13½" strips for short outer borders and two 2½" x 17½" strips for long outer borders.
- From black plaid, cut two 5½" x 9" rectangles for hanging tabs.

Embroidery and Appliqués

1. Use patterns on pages 40 and 41 to trace words onto four osnaburg pieces, positioning letters as shown in photo.
2. Backstitch words with two strands of black floss; work French knots for dots. Backstitch ground line on bear block with two strands of brown floss and on cabin block with two strands of white floss. Cut out embroidered blocks on pencil lines.
3. Reverse hat, moose, boots, cabin, tree, pond, duck, and tent patterns on pages 39, 40, and 41 and make appliqué pieces. Snow pieces on cabin are cut from doubled fabric. Fuse pieces to blocks.
4. Add embroidery stitches to the following blocks:
   - Backstitch around window panes and under chimney on cabin with two strands of black floss. Use two strands of ecru floss and a running stitch to embroider the smoke coming out of the chimney.
   - Make three cross stitches down front boot with two strands of black floss. Make a bow at top of each boot with two lazy daisy stitches and two straight stitches.
   - On remaining homespun 3½" square, place a 1¼" length of ecru cord or pearl cotton in the upper left corner to make fish block; couch in place.

Piecing and Borders

When sewing, always match right sides and raw edges and use a ¼" seam allowance.

1. Referring to photo, sew three blocks together to make top row and bottom row. To make center row, first sew two small squares together vertically. Then sew "fish stories" block and cabin block to either side.
2. Sew three rows together, matching seams where necessary.
3. Sew one short inner border to each side of pieced block. Sew one long inner border to top and bottom of pieced block. Repeat with outer borders to complete wall hanging top.

Finishing

1. Cut batting and backing the same size as wall hanging top. Sew wall hanging together.

2. Quilt in the ditch around center block, inner borders, and each pieced block.

3. Remove fish shape from fishing lure and glue to bottom of "fish stories" block.

4. Tack earring hook to bottom of couched fishing line on fish block. Cut three 8" pieces of six strand floss in different colors. Thread one color at a time in needle and take a small stitch above hook, leaving both ends on top. Repeat with remaining pieces in same hole. Tie ends together in a knot; trim ends to $1/2$". Use needle tip to separate strands.

5. In same manner, make two "lures" on hat, using two colors on each instead of three.

6. Sew bead to duck for eye.

7. For tree, cut seven $1/2$" x 4" strips from green homespun. Tie each around twig, side by side. Trim ends to shape tree slightly. Glue to right side of bear block, knot side down.

8. Paint wooden pieces as follows:
- bear — medium brown
- fish — medium green
- canoe — cream

Use stencil brush to shade as follows:
- bear — dark brown around edges
- fish — light green on belly and tail
- canoe — medium brown at top

Add white dots to top of fish. Make a black dot on fish and bear for eye. Outline bear and canoe with permanent marker. Glue wooden pieces to appropriate blocks as shown in photo.

9. Make hanging tabs from black plaid rectangles. Attach to top of wall hanging with tan buttons.

10. For hanging rod, attach a sawtooth hanger to each end of branch on back. (Be sure branch is straight enough to touch wall at ends.) Slip branch through tabs.

Basic Tools and Supplies (see page 26)

Fabrics
- Small pieces of assorted colored prints, including tan and ivory
- $1/4$ yd black solid (23 cm)
- $1/4$ yd red novelty print (23 cm)
- $5/8$ yd backing (58 cm)

Other Supplies
- Black, gold, and white embroidery floss
- Batting
- 2" x 4" fleece
- Cosmetic blush
- Permanent fabric adhesive
- $3/8$" dia. wooden plug
- Dark flesh acrylic paint
- Tacky craft glue
- Three $3/4$" dia. black buttons for "O's"
- Two $1/2$" dia. black buttons for snowman
- Two $3/16$" dia. black buttons for Santa's eyes
- $7/8$" dia. white button for "O" in "Joy"
- Three $1/2$" dia. red buttons for tree
- $3/8$" x $1/2$" black oval button for reindeer's nose
- Five 3mm dia. black beads for reindeer, snowman, and bird eyes
- Liquid fray preventative
- Two $3/4$" dia. plastic rings

Read Basic Instructions, pages 27-29.

Block and Border Preparation
- On ivory print, draw a $6^{1}/_{2}$" square for Santa block.
- On tan print, draw a $3^{1}/_{2}$" square for "Joy."
- From assorted color prints, cut five $3^{1}/_{2}$" squares and three $3^{1}/_{2}$" x $6^{1}/_{2}$" rectangles for blocks.
- From black solid, cut two 1" x $12^{1}/_{2}$" strips for short inner borders, two 1" x $13^{1}/_{2}$" strips for long inner borders, two 1" x $17^{1}/_{2}$" strips for short outer borders, and two 1" x $18^{1}/_{2}$" strips for long outer borders.
- From red print, cut two $2^{1}/_{2}$" x $13^{1}/_{2}$" strips for short center borders and two $2^{1}/_{2}$" x $17^{1}/_{2}$" strips for long center borders.

Embroidery and Appliqués
1. Use pattern on page 43 to trace three "H's" down right side of ivory square, $3/4$" from pencil line, leaving space for buttons.
2. Trace "J" and "Y" on tan square, leaving space in center for button.
3. Backstitch all letters with two strands of black floss. Cut out embroidered blocks on pencil lines.
4. Reverse reindeer, Santa, mitten, stocking, snowman, bird, tree, and star patterns on pages 42 and 43 and make appliqués. Snowman, reindeer antlers, Santa beard, and Santa hat trim are all cut from doubled fabric. Fuse all pieces except reindeer in place.
5. Add embroidery stitches to the following pieces:
   - Backstitch snowman's smile with two strands of black floss.
   - Backstitch snowline on snowman block with two strands of white floss.
   - Make snowflakes with one strand of white floss by working eight straight stitches converging at one center point. Make a French knot with two strands of white floss in center of straight stitches to finish.
   - Backstitch bird's legs with two strands of gold floss; make three straight stitches for each foot.
   - Backstitch short line for Santa's arm with two strands of black floss.

Piecing and Borders
When sewing, always match right sides and raw edges and use a $1/4$" seam allowance.
1. Referring to photo, sew three blocks together to make top row and bottom row. To make center row, first sew two small squares together vertically. Then sew snowman block and Santa block to either side.
2. Sew three rows together, matching seams where necessary.
3. Sew one short inner border to each side of pieced center block. Sew one long inner border to top and bottom of pieced center block. Repeat with center borders and again with outer borders to complete wall hanging top.
4. Fuse reindeer in place, with antlers overlapping the borders. Backstitch line down bottom of reindeer face with two strands of black floss.

Finishing

1. Cut batting and backing the same size as wall hanging top. Sew wall hanging together.
2. Quilt in the ditch around center block, inner and center borders, and each pieced block.
3. To make Santa's mustache, trace pattern, page 42, on wrong side of desired fabric. Fold fabric in half, right sides facing, with pattern on top, and place over fleece. Pin all three layers together and sew on traced lines. Cut out $1/4$" from seam; clip curves and points. Make a slash **through one fabric layer only** where indicated on pattern. Turn inside out. Tightly gather center of mustache with matching thread; knot. Apply blush to cheeks and glue mustache in place with fabric adhesive.
4. Paint wooden plug dark flesh. Use craft glue to adhere to Santa face above mustache for nose.
5. Refer to photo to sew buttons and beads to appliqués.
6. To complete snowman's scarf, cut a $5/8$" x $4^1/2$" strip from scarf fabric. Fringe $1/2$" at both ends. Apply liquid fray preventative to long edges and let dry. Tie in center and glue knot to side of snowman's neck.
7. Sew one plastic ring to each top corner of wall hanging on back, being careful not to sew all the way through to the front of the wall hanging.

HOME SWEET HOME

Finished Size: 15¹/₂" x 21¹/₂"

Basic Tools and Supplies (see page 26)

Fabrics
- ³/₈ yd white weaver's cloth (35 cm)
- ¹/₈ yd yellow print (12 cm)
- ¹/₄ yd blue plaid homespun (23 cm)
- ¹/₈ yd blue print (12 cm)
- ¹/₂ yd backing (46 cm)
- Small pieces of green print, blue and white print, and yellow print

Other Supplies
- Blue and white embroidery floss
- Batting
- Four ¹/₂" dia. white buttons
- Two ⁵/₈" dia. white buttons
- Permanent fabric adhesive
- Two ³/₄" dia. plastic rings

Read Basic Instructions, pages 27-29.

Block and Border Preparation
- On white weaver's cloth, draw a 10¹/₂" x 16¹/₂" rectangle with pencil for center block.
- From yellow print, cut two 1¹/₄" x 10¹/₂" strips for short inner borders and two 1¹/₄" x 18" strips for long inner borders.
- From blue plaid, cut two 2¹/₂" x 12" strips for short outer borders and two 2¹/₂" x 22" strips for long outer borders.

Embroidery and Appliqués
1. Draw a line with air soluble pen 1⁵/₈" in from pencil line on white fabric. Use patterns on page 44 to trace words onto line all around rectangle as shown in photo.
2. Backstitch letters with two strands of blue floss; work French knots for dots.
3. Reverse patterns on page 44 and make letters for "HOME" from blue print. Center letters on block and fuse in place.
4. Blanket stitch around each letter with three strands of white floss.
5. Cut out embroidered block on pencil lines.

Borders
When sewing, always match right sides and raw edges and use a ¹/₄" seam allowance.
1. Sew one short inner border to each side of center block. Sew one long inner border to top and bottom of center block.
2. Repeat with outer borders to complete wall hanging top.

Finishing
1. Cut batting and backing the same size as wall hanging top. Sew wall hanging together.
2. Quilt in the ditch around center block and inner borders.
3. To make yo-yo flowers, use patterns on page 45. Cut two larger circles from yellow print and four smaller circles from blue print. Fold raw edge of each circle ¹/₈" to wrong side. Using matching thread, sew running stitches around entire circle near folded edge. With right side of fabric facing out, pull thread to tightly gather fabric; knot thread to secure. Flatten yo-yo so that gathered circle is at the center. Using the larger buttons for the larger flowers, sew buttons over center holes with thread to match yo-yo.
4. To make leaves, trace leaf pattern, page 45, on wrong side of green print four times. Fold fabric in half, right sides facing, with pattern lines on top. Sew on lines, leaving open at bottom. Cut out ¹/₄" from seam; trim points. Turn right side out and press. Gather or pleat open end.
5. Center yellow flowers above and below HOME. Arrange a blue flower on either side and a leaf at each end. Glue each flower and leaf in place, overlapping edges a little.
6. Sew one plastic ring to each top corner of wall hanging on back, being careful not to sew all the way through to the front of the wall hanging.

"SEW CRAZY" SAMPLER

Finished Size: 18" x 18"

Basic Tools and Supplies (see page 26)

Fabrics
- ⅛ yd white weaver's cloth (12 cm)
- Small pieces of assorted red, green, blue, yellow, black, brown, and grey prints
- ⅛ yd blue print (12 cm)
- ¼ yd red floral print (23 cm)
- ⅛ yd green print (12 cm)
- ⅝ yd backing (58 cm)
- Small piece of red solid

Other Supplies
- Black, red, blue, yellow, and green embroidery floss
- 12" piece of red cord or pearl cotton
- Batting
- Fiberfill stuffing
- Scrap of green felt
- Colored head straight pins (about seven)
- Wire cutters
- Tacky craft glue
- Brass scissors and thimble charms
- Permanent fabric adhesive
- Six assorted buttons in bright colors
- Three ⅝" long wooden spools
- 2" dia. wooden disk
- Flesh, dark flesh, black, white, pink, and blue acrylic paints
- 40" light brown loopy doll hair
- Wooden bamboo skewer
- Two ¾" dia. plastic rings

Read Basic instructions, pages 27-29.

Block and Border Preparation
- On white weaver's cloth, draw three 3½" x 6½" rectangles with pencil for lettered blocks.
- From assorted red, green, yellow, and blue prints, cut four 3½" squares for decorated blocks, eight 2" squares for patchwork blocks, and one 6½" square for sewing machine appliqué.
- From blue print, cut two 1" x 12½" strips for short inner borders and two 1" x 13½" strips for long inner borders.
- From red floral, cut two 2½" x 13½" strips for short center borders and two 2½" x 17½" strips for long center borders.
- From green print, cut two 1" x 17½" strips for short outer borders and two 1" x 18½" strips for long outer borders.

Embroidery and Appliqués
1. Use patterns on pages 46 and 47 to center and trace words onto each of three white rectangles.
2. Backstitch all letters with two strands of black floss; work French knots for dots.
3. Arrange two sets of four 2" squares to make two four-patch blocks. For each block, sew the top two squares together on one side and the bottom two squares together on one side. Matching seams, sew pieced squares together on one long edge.
4. Reverse sewing machine patterns on page 47 and make appliqués. Make heart and three 1¼" squares for patches also. Fuse heart to one 3½" block, three overlapping patches to another 3½" block, and sewing machine to 6½" block.
5. Use two strands of black floss to blanket stitch around heart appliqué and to make random straight stitches around patches.
6. To make "thread" on sewing machine, thread a needle with cord or pearl cotton and make a few stitches across appliquéd spool. Come out at one side of spool with cord and drape across top of machine and down front. Couch cord in a few places to hold shape. Use a straight stitch with four strands of black floss for the needle, going over red cord. Clip cord and leave end free.

Piecing and Borders
When sewing, always match right sides and raw edges and use a ¼" seam allowance.
1. Referring to photo, sew three blocks together to make top row and bottom row. To make center row, first sew two small squares together vertically. Then sew "Sew Crazy" and sewing machine blocks to either side.
2. Sew three rows together, matching seams where necessary.
3. Sew one short inner border to each side of pieced center block. Sew one long inner border to top and bottom of center block.
4. Repeat with red center borders and again with green outer borders to complete wall hanging top.

Finishing

1. Cut batting and backing the same size as wall hanging top. Sew wall hanging together.

2. Quilt in the ditch around center block, inner and center borders, and each pieced block. Quilt a diagonal line from corner to corner on four-patch blocks. Use heart pattern and air soluble pen to draw heart below "Sew Crazy" and quilt on line with black quilting thread.

3. To make pincushion, use pattern on page 46. Cut one circle from red solid fabric. Sew gathering stitches around edge. Insert a ball of fiberfill stuffing in middle of circle and pull thread to gather fabric into a ball, adding more stuffing if necessary. Knot and clip thread. Cut cap from green felt. Wrap green floss around ball twice, forming quadrants of pincushion. Place cap on top, over opening, and make a straight stitch down each leaf with green floss. If necessary, clip pins with wire cutters to make them shorter. Dip pins into craft glue and push into pincushion. Glue pincushion, scissors charm, and thimble charm to "pins and needles" block with fabric adhesive.

4. Sew assorted buttons to plain block on bottom row.

5. Apply craft glue to a spool and wrap six-strand embroidery floss around it. Repeat to make a total of three spools, one each in red, blue, and yellow. Use permanent fabric adhesive to attach spools to "Life's a Stitch" block.

6. Paint disk flesh; use stencil brush to tap dark flesh onto cheeks. Add two black dots for eyes and two white dots on cheeks for highlights. Glue head to plain block on top row with fabric adhesive.

7. For hair, cut doll hair into five 8" lengths. Wrap a piece of yarn twice around two fingers; slip off and tie center of bundle with matching thread. Repeat with remaining lengths. Apply craft glue to top of head and push center of bundle into glue. Repeat on sides of head.

8. To make pencil, cut bamboo skewer into a 2" length, including point. Paint blunt end pink for eraser and tip of point black for lead. Paint most of center section blue, leaving area near tip unpainted. Apply craft glue to pencil and slip into hair.

9. Sew one plastic ring to each top corner of wall hanging on back, being careful not to sew all the way through to the front of the wall hanging.

Basic Tools and Supplies (see page 26)

Fabrics
- ¼ yd dark pink print (23 cm)
- ⅛ yd white weaver's cloth (12 cm)
- Small piece of light pink print
- ¼ yd pink floral (23 cm)
- ½ yd backing (46 cm)

Other Supplies
- Black embroidery floss
- Batting
- Four ¾" dia. pink buttons
- 2½" dia. wooden disk
- Flesh, dark flesh, black, and white acrylic paints
- 3" of ¾" wide white eyelet lace
- Permanent fabric adhesive
- 56" blonde loopy doll hair
- Tacky craft glue
- Two ¾" dia. plastic rings

Read Basic Instructions, pages 27-29.

Block and Border Preparation
- On dark pink print, draw a 6½" square with pencil for center block.
- On white weaver's cloth, draw four 2" x 6½" rectangles with pencil for lettered borders.
- From light pink print, cut four 2" squares for corners.
- From pink floral, cut two 2½" x 9½" strips for short outer borders and two 2½" x 13½" strips for long outer borders.

Embroidery and Appliqués
1. Use alphabet on page 48 to trace letters for name and birth date on paper. Draw a line 1½" up from bottom pencil line on pink square with air soluble pen. Draw another line ¾" below first. Center and trace name on top line and birth date below.
2. Trace "cute as a" in center of each border on white fabric, leaving room for button at end.
3. Backstitch all letters with two strands of floss; work French knots for dots. Cut out embroidered blocks on pencil lines.
4. Use pattern on page 48 to make heart appliqués from dark pink print. Fuse to center of light pink squares.

Piecing and Borders
When sewing, always match right sides and raw edges and use a ¼" seam allowance.
1. Sew one embroidered block to each side of center block, positioning as shown in photo. Sew one heart corner to each end of remaining embroidered blocks, rotating direction of hearts as shown. Sew these border strips to top and bottom of center block.
2. Sew one short outer border to top and bottom of center block. Sew one long outer border to each side of center block.

Finishing
1. Cut batting and backing the same size as wall hanging top. Sew wall hanging together.
2. Quilt in the ditch around center block, inner borders, and each heart appliqué.
3. Sew a pink button to each lettered border.
4. For baby face, paint wooden disk flesh; use stencil brush to tap dark flesh onto cheeks. Make two black dots for eyes and two white dots on cheeks. Use fabric adhesive to glue lace to wrong side of face at bottom. Glue face to center block.
5. For hair, cut doll hair into seven 8" lengths. Wrap each piece twice around two fingers. Slip off fingers and wrap center of bundle with matching thread. Repeat with remaining lengths of doll hair. Apply craft glue to center top of head; push center of one doll hair bundle into glue. Glue remaining bundles on sides of head.
6. To make bow, cut a 1¾" x 6½" strip from pink floral. Fold in half lengthwise, right sides facing. Trim ends at an angle. Sew raw edges, leaving a small opening for turning. Trim points and turn right side out. Whipstitch opening closed. Fold into a bow shape; wrap center with pink thread. Glue to top of head with fabric adhesive.
7. Sew one plastic ring to each top corner of wall hanging on back, being careful not to sew all the way through to the front of the wall hanging.

For a boy baby, change colors of fabric, make hair shorter, and glue bow under face for bow tie.

cute as a

cute as a

cute as a

cute as a

Carrie Marie
9-12-00

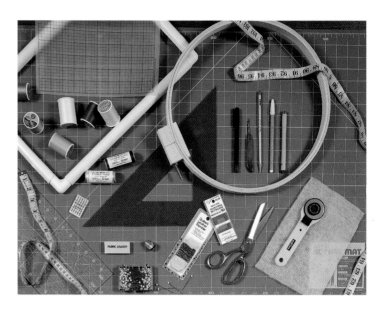

Fabrics

Choose good quality, medium weight fabrics for blocks and borders. For lettered blocks, choose weaver's cloth, osnaburg, muslin, or light-colored tone-on-tone prints.

Choose border fabrics that coordinate with stitched and appliquéd center blocks. Use contrast (color and print size) between inner and outer borders.

Rotary Cutting

18" x 24" rotary cutting mat
6" x 24" cutting ruler
Rotary cutter

Embroidering

Pencil
Light box or window during daylight hours
Tape
Air soluble pen
Embroidery floss
Embroidery hoop
Crewel embroidery needle, size 3

Piecing

Sewing machine
Straight pins
Scissors
All-purpose sewing thread in neutral color

Pressing and Appliquéing

Iron with steam and dry settings
Tracing paper
Ultra hold paper-backed fusible web
Transfer paper

Batting

Choose from regular, low-loft, and extra-loft, depending on how flat or puffy you want your wall hanging to be.

Hand Quilting

Quilting needles
Quilting thread in neutral or matching colors
Quilting hoop if desired

Machine Quilting

Walking foot or even-feed foot for sewing machine

Painting

Acrylic paints
Small flat brush for basecoating
Small stencil brush for shading
1" foam brush for wooden slats
Palette or disposable plate
Paper towels
Black permanent fine-tip marker
Stylus or toothpick
Spray matte varnish

Gluing

Permanent fabric adhesive
Tacky craft glue

BASIC INSTRUCTIONS

To make your crafting easier and more enjoyable, we encourage you to carefully read all of the basic instructions, study the color photographs, and familiarize yourself with the individual project instructions before beginning each project.

Rotary Cutting

Observe safety precautions when using the rotary cutter since it is extremely sharp. Develop a habit of retracting the blade guard **just before** making a cut and closing it **immediately afterward**, before laying down the cutter.

Use a rotary mat, ruler, and cutter to cut strips and pieces as directed in individual instructions.

Embroidering

1. Use a pencil to mark the block size on embroidery fabric according to individual project instructions. Cut at least 2" outside of marked lines in order to accommodate an embroidery hoop and to avoid fraying.
2. Tape pattern to light box or window. Place fabric over pattern and trace letters or other embroidery features onto fabric with air soluble pen.
3. Place marked fabric in embroidery hoop, separate floss strands, and hand stitch as indicated.
4. When ink has disappeared (dab water on fabric if necessary), press fabric on back and front.

STRAIGHT STITCH

FRENCH KNOT

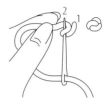

BLANKET STITCH

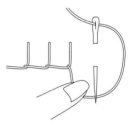

LAZY DAISY

BACKSTITCH

CROSS STITCH

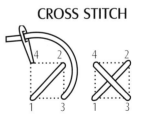

COUCHING STITCH

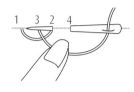

STEM STITCH

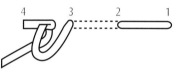

RUNNING STITCH

Piecing

Use a neutral-colored, all-purpose sewing thread (not quilting thread) in the needle and in the bobbin.

For best results, it is essential that you stitch with an accurate $\frac{1}{4}$" seam allowance. On many sewing machines, the measurement from the needle to the outer edge of the presser foot is $\frac{1}{4}$". If this is the case with your machine, the presser foot is your best guide. If not, measure $\frac{1}{4}$" from the needle and mark your throat plate with a piece of masking tape. Special presser feet that are exactly $\frac{1}{4}$" wide are also available for most sewing machines.

When piecing, always place right sides together and match raw edges; pin as necessary. Remove the pins just before they reach the sewing machine needle.

When sewing across the intersection of two seams, place pieces together, right sides facing, and match seam exactly, making sure seam allowances are pressed in opposite directions. Place a pin in the seam and one pin on either side, close to center pin, to secure placement.

Pressing

Press as you sew, taking care to prevent the small folds that sometimes form along seam lines.

Seam allowances of all borders are pressed outward. Seam allowances of pieced tops are pressed to one side. Press all seams of one row in one direction; press all seams of adjoining row to the opposite direction so that seam lines will match up accurately.

Appliquéing

When appliquéing a very light fabric over a dark fabric, it may be necessary to double the fabric. Fuse two pieces of fabric together, wrong sides facing.

1. For appliqués with a left and right direction, patterns will need to be reversed. To do this, trace the pattern onto tracing paper first; turn traced paper over and continue to follow all steps using the reversed pattern.
2. Trace the appliqué pattern onto paper side of fusible web as many times as indicated for wall hanging, leaving at least $\frac{1}{2}$" between shapes.
3. Cut about $\frac{1}{4}$" from pattern lines. Fuse web to wrong side of fabric.
4. Cut out each appliqué on drawn lines, cutting through paper and fabric. Remove paper backing.
5. Arrange appliqués, overlapping shapes as shown by dashed lines on pattern or in photo. When satisfied with arrangement, fuse in place.
6. Use transfer paper to add detail lines to finished appliqués.

Preparing to Quilt

1. Follow project instructions to cut fabric backing and batting for wall hanging.
2. Examine wrong side of wall hanging top closely; trim any seam allowances and clip any threads that may show through to the front of the wall hanging top. Press the wall hanging top.
3. Place top and backing right sides together. Lay both pieces on top of batting and pin all three layers together.
4. Sew all around, leaving a 5" opening at center bottom for turning. Trim batting close to seam; clip corners. Turn right side out through opening. Press along outer seam edge. Fold in seam allowance at opening and whipstitch closed.
5. Baste layers together through center of each border. If additional quilting is to be added, as in the pieced tops, pin or baste close to each seam.

Quilting

Quilting holds the three layers (top, batting, and backing) of the wall hanging together and adds visual appeal. All the projects have been hand quilted, but machine quilting may be substituted as desired.
1. All the wall hangings have "in the ditch" quilting, which is quilting very close to the seam line or appliqué. This type of quilting does not need to be marked and should be stitched on the side opposite the seam allowance where there is less bulk.
2. The quilt stitch is a basic running stitch through all three layers that forms a broken line on the quilt top and backing. Rock the needle up and down, taking three to six stitches before bringing the needle and thread completely through the layers. Stitches should be straight and even. Use a quilting needle and quilting thread; the use of a quilting hoop is optional.

Making Hanging Tabs

1. Cut fabric rectangles as directed. Fold each in half lengthwise, right sides together, and sew a $1/4$" seam along raw edges, leaving a small opening for turning. Clip corners and turn right side out. Press. Fold in seam allowance at opening and whipstitch closed.
2. Fold one tab in half crosswise and slip ends over top of wall hanging. Pin in position and sew a button to front tab, sewing through wall hanging and back of tab to secure. Repeat with second tab.

Painting

1. Several of the wall hangings have small wooden cut outs (available in craft stores) for dimensional embellishment.
2. Use a small, flat brush to basecoat wooden cut outs. Use a foam brush to paint or stain wooden slats. Apply additional coats as necessary for good coverage, letting dry between coats.
3. For shading edges of wooden pieces and for cheeks, dip a small stencil brush into paint. Remove excess paint on paper towel. Tap brush on painted piece until sufficient paint is applied.
4. For details, use a permanent marker to draw outlines. To make round dots for eyes or highlights, dip stylus or toothpick into paint; touch to piece. Repeat to make another dot the same size. Re-touch without reloading with paint to make smaller dots.
5. When all paint and ink is dry, spray items with two light coats of matte finish, letting dry between coats.

Warm Hands
Warm Heart

Friendship is a work of Heart

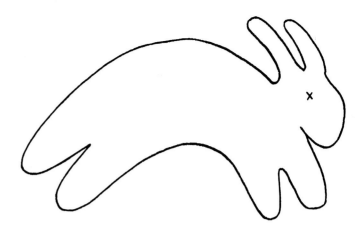

give me
the
Simple Life

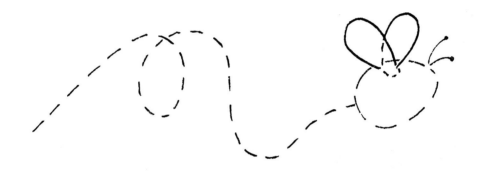

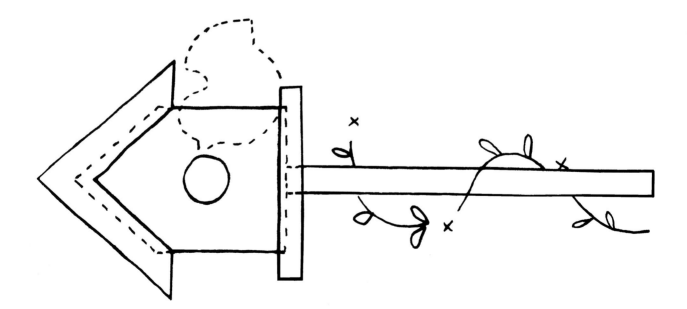

One flag, one land
One heart, one hand
One nation,
Evermore

O.W. Holmes

#1

#2

#3

#4

#5

Love is so nice

to Come home to

HAPPY

36

makes me[ll Batty *

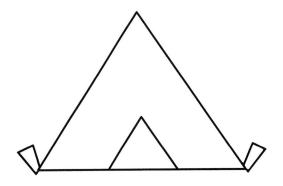

39

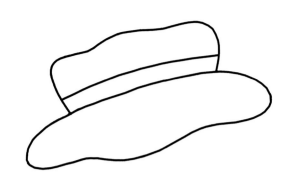

fish
stories
told
here

moose
crossing

B'ar Country

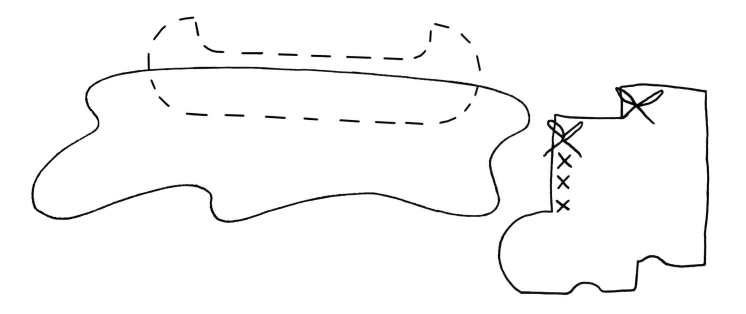

cabin fever

Sweet home ... S

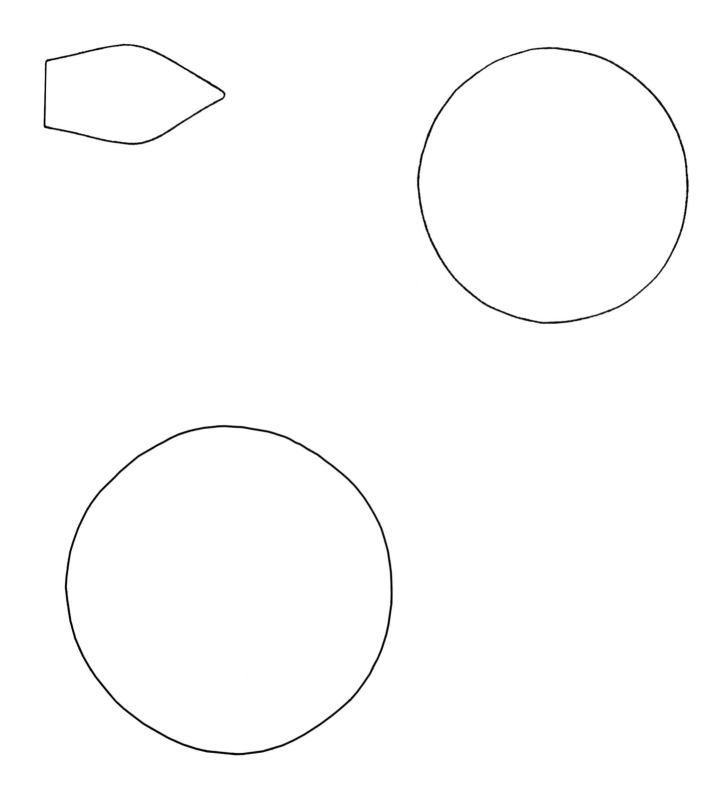

Sew Crazy

Life's a Stitch

pins and needles

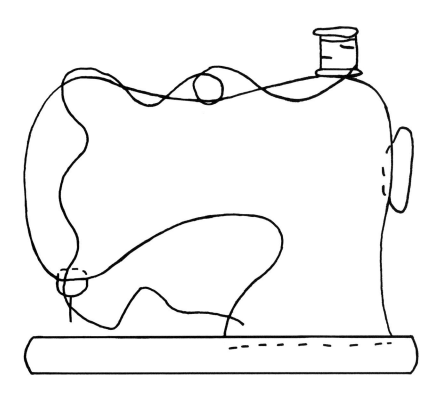

a b c d e f g h i j k l
m n o p q r s t u v w
x y z

A B C D E F G H I J K L
M N O P Q R S T U V
W X Y Z

1 2 3 4 5 6 7 8 9 0

cute as a

Production Team: Technical Writer – Michelle James; Editorial Writer – Suzie Puckett; Production Artist – Lora Puls.